For my favorite Sparky fans: Zack, Emma, Matthew, and Benjamin —B. G.

Acknowledgments:
My gratitude to Jeannie Schulz, who opened her heart to me and shared the latest writings about Sparky; to Monte, Craig, Amy, and Jill, who also shared insights about their dad. They made it a joy for me to write about Charles Schulz and his *Peanuts* kids.

I would like to give special thanks to Lisa Monhoff, archivist at the Charles M. Schulz Museum and Research Center, Santa Rosa, California, and to Laura Davis at United Feature Syndicate, Inc. They were invaluable in locating material to be included in the book.

Page 122 constitutes a continuation of the copyright page.

Library of Congress Cataloging-in-Publication Data
Gherman, Beverly.
Sparky : the life and art of Charles Schulz / by Beverly Gherman.
p. cm.
ISBN 978-0-8118-6790-0
1. Schulz, Charles M. (Charles Monroe), 1922–2000. 2. Cartoonists—United States—Biography. I. Title.
PN6727.S3Z68 2010
741.5'6973—dc22
[B]
2009005814

Book design by Jennifer Bostic, Paper Plane Studio.
Typeset in Omnes.

Manufactured by Toppan Leefung, Da Ling Shan Town, Dongguan, China, February 2011

10 9 8 7 6 5 4 3 2

This product conforms to CPSIA 2008.

Chronicle Books LLC
680 Second Street, San Francisco, California 94107
www.chroniclekids.com

Previous page / SPARKY WITH CHARLIE BROWN / C. 1958

SPARKY

The Life and Art of Charles Schulz
BY BEVERLY GHERMAN

chronicle books · san francisco

TABLE OF CONTENTS

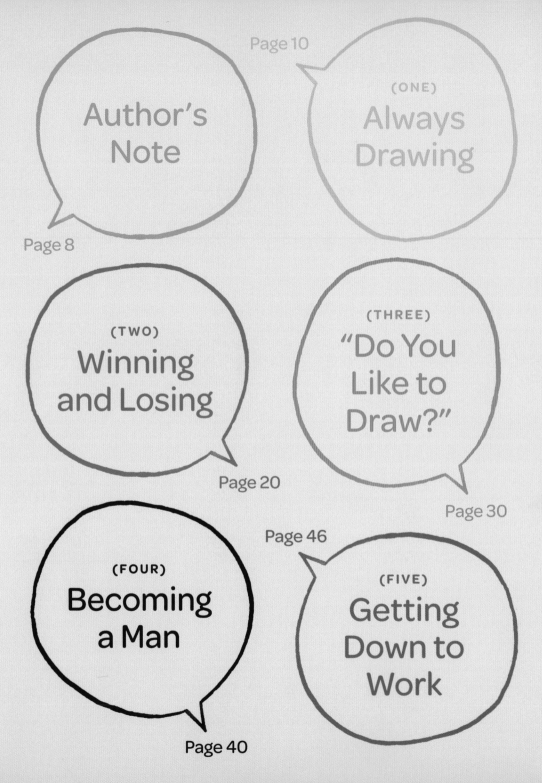

Author's Note

While I was in college, the *Peanuts* comic strip was the first thing I read in the morning's newspaper. Without fail, Charles Schulz seemed to capture my daily worries. He knew the way people of all ages suffer. Although his characters were young kids, they were struggling with popularity problems, poor grades on school tests, and misunderstandings between friends, just as I was. I could have made appointments at the counseling center on campus to get advice, but how much better to find my answers in *Peanuts*, along with a smile or laugh.

   Who was this Charles Schulz, the man who created the *Peanuts* cartoon strips for fifty years? How I wish I had known him! Instead I read about him, talked to his family and friends, and, best of all, read his strips and books and watched his videos. Through them all, I discovered how kind and generous and hardworking he was. He was born with a great talent but he never took it for granted. Throughout his life he always tried to improve his original ability.

(ONE)
Always Drawing

From the beginning, Charles Schulz intended to draw cartoons. Not just any cartoons—the very best cartoons.

He drew all the time. No matter where he was, he pulled out a stubby pencil and a wrinkled piece of paper so he could sketch a friend or copy a picture from the latest Big Little Books he collected. He noticed the way an arm popped out of a friend's shoulder or the way his collar curved around his neck. From his books he observed the way Popeye's muscles rippled under his rolled-up shirtsleeve or the way he gobbled up his spinach. Observing was just as important as drawing. He called it "mental drawing."

Charles Monroe Schulz was born on November 26, 1922. Before he was a week old, his uncle nicknamed him "Sparky." For some reason the baby reminded him of Sparky, the sad-eyed horse from the popular comic strip *Barney Google* who uexpectedly became the big winner of a race. Yet, "Sparky" stuck, and it turned out to be the perfect nickname for a talented boy who loved comic strips and who would become a winner in the cartoon world.

When Sparky was a kid, everybody—children and adults—read comics. There was no television and no electronic games. Even Sparky's parents liked comics. And while they didn't know anything about the comics business, they thought Sparky's drawings were good, and they encouraged him to follow his dreams.

Although Sparky's parents only had third-grade educations, they both were hardworking, sensible people. Carl Schulz opened his St. Paul, Minnesota, barbershop early in the morning and kept it open until late at night. He made thirty-five cents for each haircut and pennies more for shaves. It took many haircuts and many shaves to pay the rent.

Sparky often met his dad at the barbershop. Carl was always happy to see Sparky, but he never stopped cutting a customer's hair. Or, if he was cutting Sparky's hair when an "important customer" came into the shop, Carl shooed Sparky out of the barber's chair and made him wait on the bench—sometimes with half a haircut and a great deal of embarrassment.

INSIDE CARL'S BARBER SHOP / C. 1921

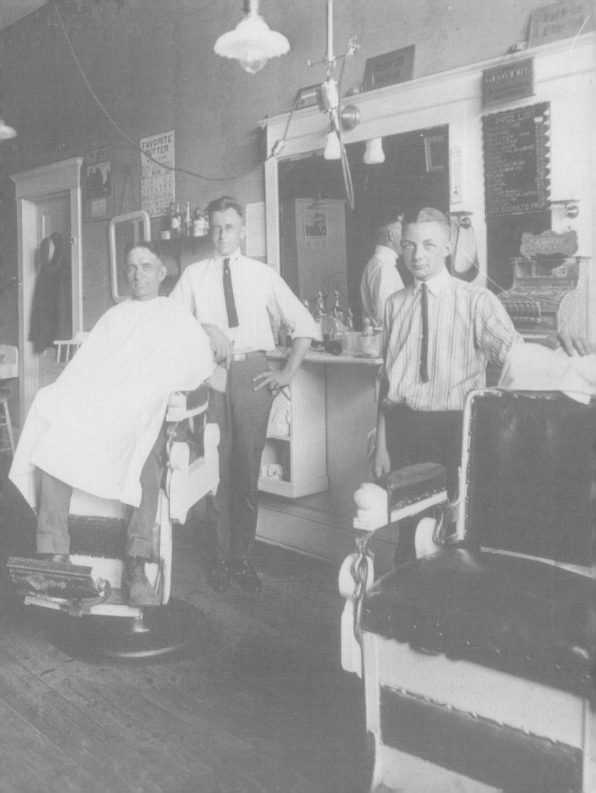

Perhaps this was when Sparky began collecting insults like other kids collected stamps. He used them later in his cartoon strips, thinking that his readers would understand those painful insults and might be able to sigh or chuckle with him.

Sparky's father even worked late on Saturday nights. Father and son would walk home together. On the way, they would stop at the nearby drugstore to pick up two Minneapolis newspapers. They loved reading the funny pages together, analyzing the comics endlessly, trying to guess what might happen next.

Often on Sunday mornings, Sparky and his parents would climb into their Ford and drive across the state line into nearby Wisconsin to visit Dena's Norwegian family at their farm.

Carl greatly valued his car. He took good care of it and was aware that not everyone could afford to own an automobile.

Dena had a reputation for making the most delicious pies. She would rise early in the day to

SPARKY RIDING HIS TRICYCLE / C. 1928

shape her flaky crust and fill it with apples or lemon curd or fresh berries to take to her family. Sparky would carry the pie on his lap all the way to the farm. He held it carefully, trying not to jiggle it too much.

Concentrating on the pie helped him avoid thinking about what was coming next. They were always greeted by barking dogs who attacked the fenders of the car and frightened Sparky. Next came the noisy cousins pulling on him to play. Sparky's mother made Sparky dress up in a freshly ironed shirt and fancy suit, even though his cousins were running about in short knickers and cotton shirts stained from grass and farm chores. He was a city kid who was not comfortable among all the animals and dirt roads of the farm. And his cousins teased him about his wanting to draw instead of going outside to play with them.

He hated those trips.

When Sparky was old enough to attend his neighborhood school, Richard Gordon Elementary School, he met other city kids like himself who wore neat, clean clothes and brown leather lace-up shoes. He fit right in.

One day, his kindergarten teacher handed out white paper and black crayons and told her students to draw anything they liked. Sparky drew a man shoveling snow. All winter long he saw bundled-up men shoveling snow in front of their homes and in their driveways. It was a familiar scene for the five-year-

old. But then he added something unexpected—a palm tree! He had certainly not seen that tree in the Minneapolis winter, but he remembered his mother reading a letter from their relatives who had moved to Southern California. They had sent a picture of the unusual palm trees they discovered there. Sparky was fascinated by the straight rough trunks of the trees and their droopy wide fronds.

Even as a kindergartner, Sparky had an unusual way of looking at the world. His teacher studied the picture. She told him, "Someday, Charles, you're going to be an artist."

TWO

Winning and Losing

In St. Paul, the Schulz family lived on a quiet street close to Carl's barbershop. When Sparky wasn't inside the apartment drawing pictures or playing with his toy cars, he was outside playing cops and robbers or cowboys and Indians with the neighborhood kids.

Sparky's best friend, Shermy Pepler, lived next door. They were both only kids, loners who had found each other. Shermy's mother played the piano and often chose music by the classical composer Beethoven, so it was natural that later Sparky's famous comic strip would feature Schroeder playing Beethoven on his toy piano. Sparky admitted that Brahms was his favorite composer, but Beethoven's name sounded funnier.

The treat of the week for Sparky and Shermy was going to the Saturday afternoon movie. First they bought popcorn for five cents at a shop down the street. Then the pair walked to the Park Theater to buy movie tickets for ten cents.

Sparky's favorite film was *Lost Patrol*, an adventure movie set in the desert with endless sand dunes and handsome figures riding their horses at top speed. He also liked cowboy and Tarzan movies. Watching films taught him how the action on the screen moved forward, scene to scene, building excitement. Later, he would use the same technique in his comic strips.

Sparky bought every comic book that he could get his hands on. He bought big black pads of plain paper and copied his favorite illustrations from the *Famous Funnies* books, *Mickey Mouse, Popeye,* and *Buck Rogers.* It was good practice, and he learned how other cartoonists shaped their characters. He read Sherlock Holmes mystery novels and drew his own mysteries.

In elementary school, Sparky caught on quickly. His teachers wanted him to skip grades so he could learn more challenging material. That worked well in the early years, but by the time he went to junior high school, he started to fall behind and never caught up. By then, he was the youngest and smallest boy in the class.

No matter how poorly Sparky was doing at school, he continued to work hard at drawing. When he was in seventh grade, he drew some political cartoons. His teacher thought they were wonderful, but she gave them to another student and asked him to make the lines darker. Sparky could draw better than most of the other kids, so he didn't understand why his teacher would let anyone else touch his work. He never got over that insult.

Working at home was different. He would move his mother's handmade crocheted tablecloth from the dining room table, lay out a newspaper, dip his pen into a bottle of black ink, and draw figures all over the cardboards he had taken from his father's laundered shirts. The ink bled into the cardboard, but that was all he had to use. Better paper cost money.

Sparky loved to tease his mother. One day, he told her he had spilled ink all over the table. She ran to get a wet towel, but she stopped when she heard him laughing. Sparky had a sense of humor to go along with his drawing talent. He always told people,

"There are no artists in the family, but there are a lot of funny people."

In addition to being a good artist, Sparky was a good athlete. During the frigid Minnesota winters, Sparky's father flooded the backyard so it would freeze over and the kids could skate and play hockey.

When there was no ice, Sparky practiced hockey in the basement using tennis balls instead of a puck. He'd ask his grandmother to play goalie, and she'd keep her broom in constant movement to keep him from scoring.

Sparky also loved baseball. He and the neighbor kids played on vacant lots. In those days, there were no official Little Leagues. The kids came to the lot with cracked bats and balls held together with black electrical tape, but they always had fun.

One summer, when Sparky was fourteen, a playground manager organized four teams to play each other. The first game started at nine in the morning but Sparky arrived at seven thirty because he was so eager to play. In the games, Sparky switched from pitcher to catcher, depending on which position was needed.

SPARKY WITH HIS DAD, A SLED, AND THEIR DOG / C. 1927

During one amazing game, Sparky pitched a no-hit shutout and his team won the championship. Winning felt wonderful. Soon afterward, the team lost a game 40–0. That didn't feel as good, but it made for a funnier story.

In high school, Sparky's classmates weren't as impressed with his drawing skills as they had been in elementary school. Back then, they had clamored for him to draw Popeye or other figures on their notebooks. But as they grew older, his classmates became interested in other things, like dating and girls. Sparky didn't ask girls out on dates. He was skinny as a rail and had pimples all over his face. "Who'd want to date me?" he asked himself. He couldn't wait to graduate and be done with school.

When Sparky was a senior in high school, a teacher asked him to create some cartoons for the yearbook. When he got his copy of the book, he searched each page for his drawings, but they were not included. "That was a crushing blow," he said, almost forty years later.

Fortunately, he did not stop drawing. His art teacher in high school, Miss Paro, was impressed with his work and encouraged him to keep at it.

In one assignment, Sparky had illustrated trios of everyday items: golf clubs, coffee cups, cemetery head stones, artists' palettes, dollar bills, roller skates. He raced through his drawings while the other students were still trying to think of what to draw. Miss Paro felt that Sparky's mind was "working every minute." He never turned it off.

Many years later, a writer, Dan Shanahan, compared Sparky's trio of golf bags to master painter Rembrandt's paintings of individual leaves on trees. Shanahan had told Sparky his drawings depicted the same whimsy and beauty. Sparky was pleased to have "someone compare [his] work with Rembrandt's."

(THREE)

"Do You Like to Draw?"

Sparky's parents encouraged him to keep working on his drawing in any way they could. When Sparky was fourteen, they took him to see an exhibit of original cartoons at a St. Paul library. As Sparky walked from one cartoon to the next, he compared his work to the drawings before him. He saw how finished and professional their cartoons were, how sure their pen lines were compared to his own. But he also noticed their work wasn't perfect. Mistakes were covered with correction fluid or tape, and editors' comments were penciled lightly all over the pages. He realized that a finished cartoon needed many revisions. As soon as Sparky got home, he tore up all his drawings. He knew it would take more time for him to become a professional cartoonist.

Once he felt more confident, he sent some of his work to magazines and newspapers. He was first published in *Ripley's Believe It or Not!* on February 22, 1937. The drawing was of his dog Spike, with a description of all the things the dog ate.

Spike not only ate unusual things, he scared all the neighbors. He was not a big dog, but he acted like

a ferocious guard dog. When Shermy knocked on the Schulzes' door, he was afraid Spike was going to eat him. Sparky laughed at Shermy's fear and bragged that the dog never snarled or turned on him.

In his senior year of high school, Sparky's mother noticed an ad in the newspaper for Federal Schools, a correspondence school that gave instruction in drawing. The ad asked, "Do You Like to Draw?" She showed it to Sparky. "Why not fill out the form and show them how well you draw," she suggested. Sparky did.

Before long, a man from the school came to meet Sparky and his parents. He told them the course would cost $170. That was a lot of money at the time.

In St. Paul and throughout the rest of the country, money was still tight in the years following the Great Depression. Men had lost their jobs. They stood in line to get a hot meal. Businesses closed. Banks failed.

Carl asked if he could pay the amount in small installments, since he could not spare that much money at once. They worked out a payment schedule of ten dollars a month, and Sparky began the class in March 1940.

DRAW ME!

COPY THIS GIRL

$1275.00 IN PRIZES!

5 PRIZES! 5 Complete $255 Art Courses, including Drawing Outfits!

's your big chance, if you t to become a commercial st, designer, or illustrator! easy-to-try way to win EE art training!

ther you win or not we send our comments on your work, if your drawing shows promise! Trained illustrators, artists and cartoonists now making big money. Find out now if YOU have profitable art talent. You've nothing to lose—*everything to gain*. Mail your drawing today.

DON'T WORK HARD SCRA

And as tight as money was, Carl always managed to find enough for Sparky's art school.

Students sent their homework by mail and received critiques from the teachers by return mail. Because the school was located in St. Paul, Sparky could have delivered his homework in person. But he didn't. He worried the teachers might think his work was terrible. How could he stand there and watch them frown when they looked at his drawings? It was easier to mail his assignments to the school and wait for the teachers to write back to him about how he could improve. He was able to take their advice and do well in most of his classes. Ironically, he didn't do as well in the class that focused on classical ways to draw children. Perhaps even then, he had his own ideas for drawing kids.

Sparky graduated from the art school on December 1, 1941, when he was nineteen. A few days later, on December 7, 1941, the United States entered the Second World War after the Japanese bombed the United States naval fleet in Pearl Harbor, Hawaii. During the two previous years, the German army had marched into Poland and other

European countries. The United States was drawn into war in both Europe and Asia and began training young men to go overseas.

Sparky was drafted into the army in November 1942. He was twenty years old when he left for training at nearby Fort Snelling in St. Paul.

At about the same time, Sparky noticed his mother didn't have her usual energy. Dena had always been his strongest supporter. It turned out she had been ill for several years with cervical cancer. At that time, most doctors did not tell their patients when they had an incurable disease. It was thought they would get depressed and give up hope. The doctor never told Dena what was wrong or that she would not get well. Sparky didn't know anything either. He kept hoping she would get out of bed and be herself. But he heard her cries, especially during the night, when she was in pain. He hated leaving for training in the army while she was so sick.

In February 1943, Sparky got a weekend pass to visit his mother. He stood at the side of her bed and watched her fitful sleep. Even Spike wasn't allowed to lie on her bed any longer because his movement

SPARKY, HIS PARENTS, AND SPIKE / C. 1938

caused her pain. Dena told Sparky they should name their next dog Snoopy.

As Sparky was leaving to go back to his base, she said weakly, "I suppose we should say good-bye, because we probably never will see each other again." She died the following day. After her funeral, Sparky went back to Fort Snelling feeling so badly he cried in his bunk that night. Later, he would remember what she had told him about naming his next dog and would use the name Snoopy for his famous beagle.

SPARKY AND HIS PARENTS UPON HIS DEPARTURE FOR MILITARY TRAINING / C. 1940

FOUR

Becoming a Man

At first, Sparky was lonely in the army, but he soon made a close friend. Elmer Hagemeyer was older and had been a policeman before he joined the army. Elmer would have nothing to do with a nickname like Sparky. Instead he called his new friend Charlie. Their unit was sent to Camp Campbell in Kentucky to join the 20th Armored Division. They spent almost two years there, drilling and learning to use machine guns.

Sparky was a good machine gunner and a good leader. He was soon promoted to staff sergeant and squad leader. He was gaining confidence he had never known and building muscles he had never had. Being in the army was a positive experience for him. The only thing he couldn't adjust to was the coarse language of the other men. He tried to ignore it and made sure he never used ugly four-letter words.

When other soldiers saw Sparky sketching, they asked him to decorate the letters they sent home, just as the kids in elementary school had asked him to draw on their binders. He illustrated his own letters to his dad, making fun of himself and the other soldiers.

In February 1945, the unit was sent to Europe on the *Brazil*, a luxury liner that had been converted for military transport. It was Sparky's first opportunity to see the ocean. After thirteen days of maneuvering to avoid enemy ships in the rough waters of the Atlantic Ocean, he was ready to land in France.

From Rouen, France, they traveled to Germany in a half-track, a ten-ton fighting vehicle, large enough to hold his eleven-man squad. The wheels were covered with steel traction to keep the heavy half-track from getting stuck in mud. The men nicknamed it Sparky. Their orders were to prevent the Germans from blowing up any more bridges, so that the United States and the rest of the Allied Forces could move into Germany.

Once, in a German village, Sparky found a suspicious barracks he thought might be a hiding place for enemy soldiers. He took a grenade from his belt and was ready to throw it into the doorway. Suddenly, a small dog entered the building. Sparky refrained from throwing the grenade. He couldn't blow up an innocent dog. Later he said, "That dog never harmed anyone."

ARMY LETTER / C. 1944

gt. E. R Hagemeyer 37606063
B. 8th A. I Bn 20th A.D.
O. 444 Camp Campbell Ky
. Army

Mrs. E R
3655
St.

Sparky was awarded a Combat Infantryman Badge (CIB) for his excellence in combat. Throughout his life, if anyone asked him what he most valued, he always answered that the CIB was his most prized possession. It was recognized and highly regarded by other soldiers as the "fighter badge." To Sparky, it meant he had been a brave soldier.

In May 1945, the war in Europe ended. Sparky sailed back to the United States in early August. By the time he arrived in New York, an atomic bomb had been dropped on Hiroshima, Japan, on August 6, 1945. The war with Japan would soon be over. That meant he and his men would not be sent to fight against the Japanese army as they had feared.

Sparky spent his first weeks back in the United States at Camp Shanks in New York, where he was processed out of the service. Before his discharge, he spent a short time in Lompoc, California, where he played golf and enjoyed the pleasant weather. He finally returned to St. Paul at the end of the year and immediately went to the barbershop. His father greeted him but didn't stop cutting his customer's hair.

Even without the hugs of welcome, Sparky felt good about himself, and it showed in his confident appearance in photographs from those days. "I feel like somebody . . . I became a man," he said about his time in the army.

The good feelings "lasted about twelve minutes. And then I was back to being my regular self." He knew he could not continue to live on the positive memories of his army service; it was time to decide what he should do with the rest of his life.

SPARKY PLAYING BASEBALL IN THE ARMY / C. 1943

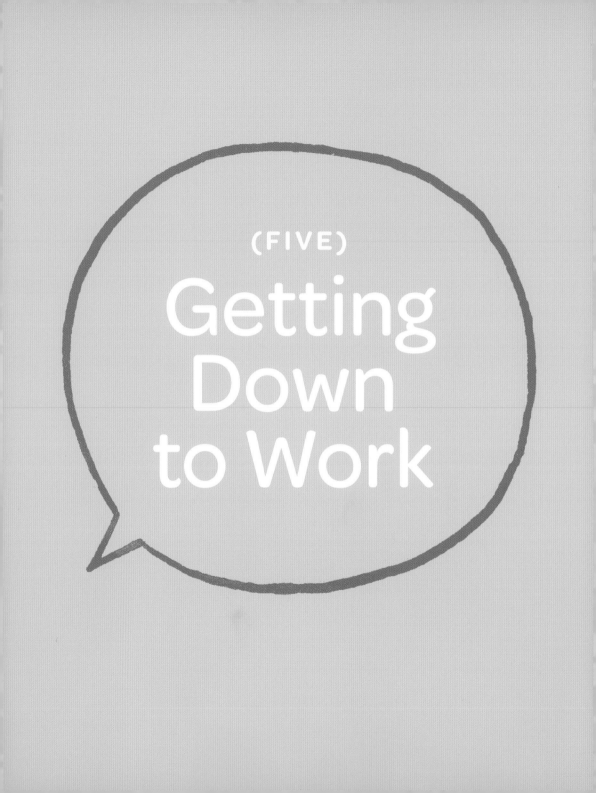

(FIVE)

Getting Down to Work

After he was discharged from the army, Sparky moved into the family apartment with his father. He looked for jobs in town and sent off samples of a war story and two other strips to a New York comics publisher. When they rejected his work, Sparky sent it to other publishers. His father worried that Sparky might never find a decent job. As he talked to his customers in the barbershop, he wondered whether his son's ambition to be a cartoonist would ever amount to anything.

Sparky finally found a job lettering comic strips for a St. Paul company that produced Roman Catholic teaching aids. They needed him to do the lettering in three languages: English, Spanish, and French. They didn't mind that Sparky couldn't speak Spanish or French. He lettered well and could simply copy the words they gave him. He was paid a dollar and fifty cents an hour.

He was also offered a job at his old correspon-dence school, which had been renamed Art Instruction Schools. He was hired to evaluate students' artwork. After studying a student's drawings, Sparky wrote his criticisms—good and bad—to the student. For that, he

CHAPTER FIVE / GETTING DOWN TO WORK

was paid thirty-two dollars per week. He and the rest of the instructors sat at adjoining desks. Sometimes they drew amusing pictures that they shared with each other, laughed about, and then threw away. After a while, his fellow instructors became his friends and best critics. They shared books and music and art. He learned a great deal from them.

He set up a studio in his parents' old bedroom, trying to erase the memory of his mother dying in that very room. He pinned up drawings by his fellow instructors and made the room his own. Often he worked late into the night completing the lettering for the Catholic comics. Most days, after working at the Art Instruction Schools in Minneapolis, Sparky took a streetcar to St. Paul to drop off the lettering work he had completed and to pick up a new batch of cartoons to letter for the following day.

During that time, Sparky was beginning to draw his own funny pictures of kids. He needed names, so he borrowed Linus from one of his friends at Art Instruction, Charlie Brown from another. He had already planned to use Shermy's name for one of the boys.

SPARKY WITH CHARLIE BROWN / C. 1958

Li'l Folks

BY SPARKY

"TIMBER !!!"

"I'LL HAVE TO TELL YOU LATER...
I CAN'T TALK NOW!"

"I FIND THAT THIS HIGH
ALTITUDE DOES WONDERS
FOR MY APPETITE."

"I'VE HAD THE AWFUL FEELING
LATELY THAT BEETHOVEN
IS GOING TO KILL ME!"

When he left samples of his work on his friends' desks, he watched to see their reactions. If he saw them laughing, that was a good sign. Most of the time, they encouraged him to keep drawing those kids. The fellows said his drawings "kept getting better" as he simplified the lines and stopped trying to add every detail.

He even had one of his drawings published in the Catholic comics. It showed a boy giving his mother a birthday present and telling her "...if you don't like it, the man said I could exchange it for a hockey puck." The day it was published was Dena's birthday, and that truly gave his success a special meaning.

Sparky continued drawing comic panels of kids and sold them to the *St. Paul Pioneer Press,* which agreed to publish a weekly comic. It appeared on the women's page, sometimes squeezed in between wedding announcements. In the strips, the girls usually complained about the boys or bashed them over their heads.

He dreamed about having one of his single-panel cartoons published in the *Saturday Evening*

LI'L FOLKS CARTOON FROM THE ST. PAUL PIONEER PRESS / 1948

Post, an extremely popular magazine sold all around the country. After sending them cartoon after cartoon, one was finally accepted. The magazine paid Sparky forty dollars.

They used his full name on the page, "Charles Schulz," instead of Sparky, but he was still Sparky to everyone who knew him. The magazine continued to publish his single-panel cartoons, but he was eager to find another newspaper or magazine that would publish his longer cartoons.

He sent cartoons to United Feature Syndicate in New York City. The syndicate marketed many important newspaper comic strips and daily columns. Sparky waited and waited to hear from them. Weeks went by. Every day he rushed to the barbershop to see if any mail had come for him.

Nothing. He was naive enough to think they would answer immediately. He had no idea they were swamped with cartoons submitted by artists from all across the country and could not answer all of them immediately. At last he received a letter from the syndicate inviting him to come to New York to show them more of his work.

(SIX)
Losing the Red-Haired Girl

On Sunday, June 11, 1950, Sparky gathered up his drawings and boarded the train to New York City. When he arrived, he registered at the Roosevelt Hotel. He was too excited to sleep that night and tossed and turned until early the next morning. With his drawings, he rushed through a drizzling rain to the syndicate offices in a skyscraper on East Forty-Second Street. It was so early that no one was there yet except the switchboard operator. She offered to hold on to his work while he had some breakfast.

Sparky came back at ten o'clock. He discovered the men had been looking at his work before he returned. They liked it but said they wanted strips rather than two-panel cartoons. They asked him if he could draw a strip and develop the characters. Of course he could, he told them. They offered him a five-year contract with a fifty-fifty split of the profits.

Without telling him, they also changed the name of the strip. They said he could not use the title Sparky had wanted, *Li'l Folks*, because another strip already had used a similar name. They liked *Peanuts*. Sparky didn't. But he had very little power at that point. And he knew it. In order to have his work published, he had to be flexible. He didn't get the name he wanted, but he had a contract. He was now a real cartoonist!

On the train back to St. Paul, he treated himself to a steak dinner. He had done it! He couldn't wait to tell Donna.

Donna Mae Johnson worked in the accounting office at the art school. She had bright red hair and lovely blue eyes. Every day, Sparky arrived at school before she did and drew cartoons on her day's appointment book so she would think of him all day. It was easier than trying to talk to her. In spite of his growing success, he still became tongue-tied in person.

Gradually he built up the courage to invite Donna on a date. He took her to an ice-skating show and to see the ballet film *The Red Shoes*. They went on a picnic together and out to dinner. Sparky found Donna easy to talk to. The more time he spent with her, the more he liked her.

In fact, Sparky liked Donna so much that he told her he wished he had an engagement ring to put on

PEANUTS
WOULDN'T IT BE SOMETHING IF I COULD BE WALKING ALONG IN THE SNOW WITH THAT LITTLE RED-HAIRED GIRL?
MAYBE SHE'D BE WEARING FURRY MITTENS, AND MAYBE WE'D CLIMB TO THE TOP OF THIS BIG HILL, AND SLIDE DOWN ON A TOBOGGAN, AND WHEN WE WERE SLIDING DOWN, MAYBE I'D PUT MY ARMS AROUND HER, AND...
WOW!
2-6
Tm. Reg. U. S. Pat. Off.—All rights reserved © 1971 by United Feature Syndicate, Inc.
NO WAY!
SCHULZ

her finger. When she agreed to elope with him, Sparky gave it some thought, and then said he couldn't do that to her parents. They would be too disappointed not to be present when she married.

One afternoon, Sparky went to Donna's house. They sat on the back porch steps and talked for a long time. He asked her to marry him in a proper wedding ceremony and told her they would live happily ever after, especially now that he had his own cartoon strip.

Donna said she had thought about it a lot, too, that she really liked him, but she couldn't marry him. She had decided to marry a man with whom she had grown up, who went to her church and knew her better than anyone in the world. Sparky was devastated. He drove around the neighborhood for a half hour and then drove back to Donna's house.

SPARKY WITH DONNA, WHO INSPIRED HIS "RED-HAIRED GIRL" IN THE STRIP / C. 1950

He rang the bell, and when Donna came to the door, her eyes were red from crying. He asked her if she had changed her mind, but she told him she was still going to marry her long-time beau.

Sparky realized he should have eloped with Donna when he had the chance and not worried about her parents' feelings. It was the kind of disappointing moment Sparky would depict over and over in his comic strips. Little did Donna know, she would become his idealized red-haired girl.

Sparky had learned that good guys don't always win. Later he would say that Charlie Brown's personality was born at that moment.

(SEVEN)

Growing
Peanuts

On October 2, 1950, Sparky's first *Peanuts* strip ran in seven newspapers, including the local *Star Tribune of Minneapolis* and national papers like the *Washington Post* and *Seattle Times.* That day, he went out with one of his friends from the art school to buy all seven papers at a nearby newsstand. The vendor didn't know what they were talking about when they asked for the papers carrying *Peanuts.* "We don't sell peanuts!" the guy said. That made Sparky dislike the name of his strip even more. But when they finally found the right newspapers, it was amazing to see his strip in all of them, no matter what it was called.

Everyone commented on how unique *Peanuts* was. It looked different than any other strip. It was not an action strip like *Dick Tracy* or *Steve Canyon,* whose characters were trying to solve world affairs or criminal cases. *Peanuts* was not cluttered with details. Sparky left white space so that his characters stood out. There was a horizon line, a few steps or maybe a curb for the kids to sit on.

THE FIRST *PEANUTS* STRIP, "HERE COMES CHARLIE BROWN" / 1950

Gradually, more newspapers added the *Peanuts* comic strip. The goal of the syndicate was to reach one hundred papers. Then it would mean the strips were making enough money to bring in a profit for the syndicate and for Sparky.

There were only four children in the early strips: Charlie Brown, Shermy, Patty, and Violet. Plus Snoopy. Soon baby Schroeder was included. The following year the strip ran in twenty papers and in 1952 the Sunday strip was added—in color.

Sparky showed his characters trying to solve problems. In those early strips, the story revolves around Charlie Brown. He worries because the girls are always picking on him. He wants to be tougher. In one strip, Violet wants to make a delicious mud pie, but nothing she adds tastes right. In another strip, Patty worries that she isn't pretty. And Snoopy, the observer, watches the kids dealing with their daily concerns.

In the fall of 1950, Sparky attended a party at the art school, where he met a friend's sister, Joyce Halverson. He already had dated both of her older sisters. He especially liked their mother, Dorothy.

The sisters teased him that he really wanted Doro-thy to be his mother because he loved her pancakes.

Joyce was divorced and had a one-year-old daughter, Meredith. When they started dating, Sparky was a bit overwhelmed by Joyce. Whereas Joyce was fun loving and had lots of energy, Sparky was quiet and restrained. But they shared an appreciation of music, and before Sparky knew it, he was in love.

After dating a little more than six months, Sparky and Joyce married on April 18, 1951, at the home of Joyce's cousin in Minneapolis, overlooking picturesque Minnehaha Creek. He quickly adopted Meredith. Right after their wedding, Sparky's father married his girlfriend, Annabelle. Carl said he had waited to see Sparky married first because he "didn't want to leave [his son] alone." They all lived together in Annabelle's house in St. Paul, where Sparky worked on his strips on a card table in the basement.

It wasn't a perfect situation and before long, Joyce felt the need to get away from their humdrum Minnesota life and have time with her new husband.

She convinced Sparky they should move to Colorado Springs, where they had spent their honeymoon. Sparky was desolate. He didn't want to leave his friends, his father, and everything he knew in St. Paul. He liked his familiar life. It was comforting. Anything new terrified him. But he wanted to please his wife.

Colorado Springs was rugged country surrounded by mountains. They moved into a small house in Bonneville, a new suburb of look-alike homes with low payments, perfect for a young army vet. The view of massive Pikes Peak through their living room window didn't cost a cent. Joyce was in seventh heaven, because she could jump on a horse and ride for miles to get away from civilization. Sparky tried to work at home, but there were too many distractions inside and outside the house. Meredith was into everything, and the yard needed his attention. He finally realized he had to get an office.

He found a place downtown with no phone, no people, and no beautiful views to distract him. There he set up his drafting board, pulled out his pencil, his pen, and his bottle of India ink, and got to work. His method became to doodle on yellow lined paper until he had a possible idea for the strip. Once ideas were set in his mind, he took paper preprinted with four panels and made a few pencil lines to be sure his words would fit properly.

Surprisingly, Sparky inked the speech balloons first. Many cartoonists penciled in their whole strips and then inked over the lines. Not Sparky. He drew the characters with a pen—his C-5 Speedball nib—because he liked shaping them with a pen line, not copying over pencil lines. That kept his lines fresh and free.

He had worked hard to learn pen techniques while studying at the correspondence school when he was a young man. He continued to perfect his lines as a surgeon works to perfect his surgical skills. In later years, Sparky described the joy he felt when he brought the pen down and made a drawing of Linus— or any of the other kids—with his messy hair and his striped T-shirt. He knew he had made the best pen line he could make.

Now that he had a quiet office, Meredith's nonstop activity was an inspiration rather than a

Next page / SPARKY DRAWING THE "I HATE SCHOOL" STRIP / C. 1969

distraction. Before long, he created a new character, Lucy, who had many of Meredith's qualities and energized the strip. Lucy stirs things up. She shouts! She says outrageous things to all the kids; she especially taunts Charlie Brown. She seems to know how to irritate him or get under his skin. She understands how sensitive he is and uses that against him. For Lucy's outsized comments, Sparky switched to a broader pen nib, so that he could express her strong personality.

Sparky and Joyce wanted to have a larger family. Their first son was born in February 1952. They named him Charles Monroe Schulz, Jr. and called him Monte. Soon, Lucy had a baby brother, too—Linus was added to the strip.

They made friends with a young couple, Fritz and Lou Van Pelt, who lived nearby. The four of them spent evenings having dinner and then playing cards. Sparky borrowed their last name, Van Pelt, for the characters Lucy and Linus.

But even with new friends, Sparky was not happy in Colorado Springs. He convinced Joyce to move back to Minnesota. In March 1952, after

PEN NIB THAT SPARKY USED FOR HIS STRIPS

nine months in Colorado Springs, they packed up everything and headed back to Minneapolis. Sparky quickly settled into his familiar life. He and Joyce had two more children: Craig was born in January 1953 and Amy in August 1956.

Sparky's work continued to flourish. His earnings increased to $2,500 a month at a time when most people were earning only $350. A publishing company agreed to publish a book of *Peanuts* strips that had previously appeared in the paper. And the strip found a new audience on college campuses. Professors used them in psychology textbooks, and college kids read the strip every day, searching for answers to their own personal problems. Most of all, readers enjoyed Sparky's subtle humor and wise understanding of human behavior. A psychiatrist, who regularly read *Peanuts* said that Sparky was "one of the most gifted and insightful observers of human behavior known to us."

By the summer of 1955, *Peanuts* was running in one hundred newspapers.

EIGHT

They Like Me!

On April 13, 1955, the family moved to a large home on West Minnehaha Parkway in Minneapolis. The house was luxurious with six bedrooms and a playroom for the children, as well as a finished basement with a pool table. There was a huge front lawn facing the parkway, and the surrounding homes were as tall and impressive as theirs.

Once a year, the National Cartoonists Society selected a cartoonist to win the Reuben Award. The bronze trophy, designed by Rube Goldberg, a creative cartoonist, resembles a jumble of cartoonists flowing from an ink bottle.

In 1956, Sparky went to New York to attend the society's banquet. During the meal and throughout friendly banter at the table, Sparky could think about only one thing.

When Rube Goldberg stood to announce the winner, the room grew quiet and Sparky held his breath. And then, he heard Goldberg say that Charles Schulz was the winner of the Reuben Award. He was the cartoonist of the year. It's easy to imagine thirty-three-year-old Sparky, wearing a dignified black

tuxedo on the outside, while in his head there was a kid shouting, "They like me! They really like me!"

Sparky hurried up to the front of the room to receive his Reuben. Not only did his fellow cartoonists like him, they thought he was one of the best. And he had been creating his *Peanuts* strips for only five years. Nine years later, in 1964, he won the Reuben again and became the first cartoonist to win it twice.

Winning the Reuben did not change Sparky's life or make him want to relax or take time off. In fact, it encouraged him to work harder to find new stories to delight his readers.

But Joyce found it harder and harder raising four young children in Minneapolis, especially when winter came. On with the snowsuits, mittens, hats that usually got lost, and heavy socks that would hardly fit in their boots. The children would play outside in the snow until they were too cold, and then the routine began all over again. Off with the boots, the wet socks, the mittens, the snowsuits, and maybe the hats—if they weren't lost.

Sparky and Joyce's fifth child, Jill, was born in 1958. Shortly after that, they received a letter from a neighbor who had moved to California. She told them about all the wonderful advantages of living in an area that had no snow. She was especially excited about the orange tree in her front yard. Every morning, she could pick the fruit from her tree and make her own orange juice. Sparky also had fond memories of his time there after the war. That did it. Joyce convinced Sparky they had to move to California.

They flew to the West Coast and searched in areas near San Francisco. Just as they were ready to return home, the Realtor took them to Sebastopol, a town north of San Francisco. They found the perfect place on Coffee Lane with room for horses and plenty of land to build a house with enough bedrooms for all of them. The area was known for its Gravenstein apple orchards. When they moved in, the friendly neighbors brought baskets of apples to welcome them. Before long, they would have apples, as well as oranges, growing around their property.

Joyce hired contractors and architects, who

went to work building the house and adding a tennis court and swimming pool. By the end of 1960, they were living in their new home and ready to celebrate the holidays without snowstorms and freezing weather. All of them thrived in their new community. The children grew up with great freedom and independence. They rode horses along the trails, or they rode motorbikes or bicycles if they were in a hurry to get someplace.

Sparky adored his children. When his daughter Amy came into the studio to talk to him, Sparky put down his pen and gave her all his attention. She said she never realized he had a job, because he was always right there for her. When his youngest daughter, Jill, became a skilled ice-skater, Sparky drove her all over the state to skating competitions. When his sons wanted him to play ball, they never hesitated to interrupt him either. He liked pitching to them or rallying with them on the tennis courts. He could always come back later to work on the strip.

As his own children were growing up, he saw how much they enjoyed television programs. But Sparky

IMAGE FROM THE CHRISTMAS TELEVISION SPECIAL, *A CHARLIE BROWN CHRISTMAS*,
FIRST SHOWN ON DECEMBER 9, 1965

Sparky had always said he would not put his *Peanuts* characters on television. He kept resisting until a local producer persuaded him to give it a try for a Christmas special. He said he would, but only if they used his ideas.

Sparky's first televised *Peanuts* program, *A Charlie Brown Christmas,* was shown on December 9, 1965. Sparky had insisted that the program be about the true meaning of Christmas. He wanted no laugh track. He insisted the roles would be played by kids using their own voices, not adults mimicking them. He wanted no exaggerated animation, such as when animals chase each other or hit each other over the head. He wanted less movement, in keeping with his daily strips. Initially, he thought traditional hymns would be perfect for the background music, but others persuaded him to try some lively jazz music, because it would add a bounce to the special.

He wrote a simple script in which Charlie Brown searches for the meaning of Christmas and finds it when Linus stands up and recites the story of the Christ child's birth, using the Gospel of St. Luke, to stress "peace and good will toward men."

He completes his explanation by saying in his quiet, gentle voice, "That's what Christmas is all about, Charlie Brown." Then all the children help Charlie Brown decorate his skinny little fir tree, which is almost falling to the ground. They make it stand tall and add ornaments until it glows with beauty.

Before it aired on television, CBS executives were worried. They were afraid the public would object to the religious aspect of the program. They expected angry phone calls and letters. How wrong they were! Instead, "All heaven broke loose," one of them later admitted. Phone calls indicated that half the country had watched the program and liked it. People were touched by the story and pleased with Vince Guaraldi's sophisticated jazz music, which brought the story to life. Newspaper critics wrote positive reviews. They found the quiet animation perfect for Sparky's characters and declared the program a classic after that very first showing. With such success, CBS asked Sparky to create four more television programs. There were holiday specials such as *It's the Great Pumpkin, Charlie Brown; Be My Valentine, Charlie Brown; A Charlie Brown Thanksgiving,* and many more television shows.

In 1966, Sparky's father, Carl, and stepmother, Annabelle, came to California for a visit. They were able to share in Sparky's delight when *A Charlie Brown Christmas* won an Emmy Award for Outstanding Children's Program. At the Hollywood ceremony, Sparky, again dressed in a tuxedo, accepted the Emmy, saying, "Charlie Brown is not used to winning, so we thank you."

After the award ceremony, Annabelle and Carl visited the family in Sebastopol. But on the morning of Sunday, May 29, Carl suddenly collapsed and died. His death was a terrible loss for Sparky. However, it helped that his father left the world knowing his son was successful and had been recognized for his ability. Sparky remembered Carl's early misgivings that he would never succeed as a cartoonist.

Next page / SPARKY WITH JILL, AMY, AND CRAIG, RIDING THE PONY CART ON CHARLIE BROWN BOULEVARD / C. 1964

NINE

Ice-Skating in Sunny California

As time passed, the kids in the *Peanuts* strip grew up and their personalities became more complex. Snoopy, the dreamer, grew more and more imaginative. In the early strips, Sparky drew Snoopy as a dog on all fours. Then Snoopy's fantasy life exploded. He stood up and became the writer, with his typewriter on top of the doghouse; the fedora-wearing lawyer, who carried his briefcase to the courthouse; the flying ace, who chased the Red Baron through the skies; and the astronaut, who beat the real astronauts to the moon. Sparky explained that when "Snoopy stood up on all fours and climbed up on his dog house, the strip took off." He had to be careful not to let Snoopy monopolize all the stories in the strip.

In 1969, the *Apollo 10* lunar expedition was sent into space as a preliminary trial for the later trip to the moon. The crew named the command module *Charlie Brown* and the lunar module *Snoopy*. They disconnected the two modules and sent *Snoopy* into orbit about eight miles above the moon to study the surface where the *Apollo 11* crew planned to land.

Just as the two modules were to reconnect, there was terrible turbulence in space. Everyone panicked. Would the modules crash into each other? From Earth, NASA scientists worked to manipulate the modules. In space, the crew did the same. Finally, the spacecraft and the lunar module were rejoined and the crew announced with great relief, "*Snoopy* and *Charlie Brown* are hugging each other."

In the strip, Sparky's Snoopy landed on the moon in March. He beat the actual astronauts on the Apollo mission, who didn't make it to the moon until July.

While Sparky worked on his comic strips, Joyce was building and creating new projects around their Sebastopol property. Her next plan was to build an ice rink in Santa Rosa after the city's rink closed. It would be for their family and all the families in the area. Sparky was enthusiastic. He loved ice-skating and playing ice hockey. The rink, formally called Redwood Empire Ice Arena and more casually called Snoopy's Home Ice, opened in April 1969 with great excitement from the community.

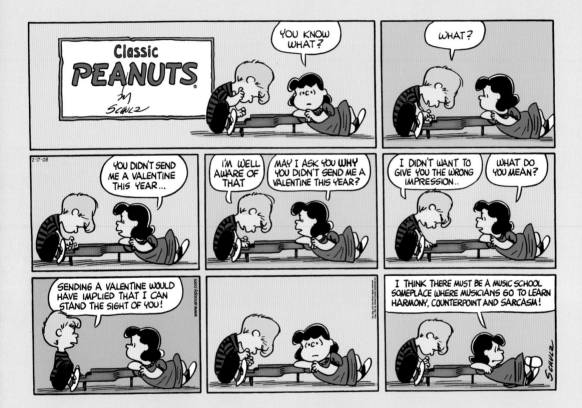

But things were not as good with the Schulz marriage. Sparky and Joyce were no longer getting along. In 1972, after twenty-one years together, they decided to divorce. Sparky felt terrible. At that time, the kids in his strips were playing baseball and Charlie Brown kicked Lucy off the team. Maybe that was what Sparky really wanted to do. But he couldn't. Instead he left the house, and started living in his office at One Snoopy Place, near the ice-skating arena.

Sparky was extremely sad. Some days he felt like a failure. But his feelings didn't keep him from drawing the *Peanuts* strip every day. Afterward, he said he had drawn some of his best strips during this time.

Soon he began eating his breakfast and lunch at the Warm Puppy Cafe next to the rink. He had a reserved table near the door, which allowed him to watch everyone come and go. He could also watch his daughters Amy and Jill while they skated.

One day, he noticed a smiling woman bringing her daughter to the rink. After she returned a few more times, he suggested she join him for a coffee at his table. Her name was Jeannie Clyde.

Sparky liked talking to her, and before long they discovered they were meant to be together. "Sparky swept me off my feet," Jeannie said later.

Sparky and Jeannie were married in September 1973, surrounded by all their children. Hers: Brooke and Lisa. His: Meredith, Monte, Craig, Amy, and Jill.

In 1974, Sparky was asked to serve as Grand Marshal for the Tournament of Roses Parade in Pasadena, California. The parade is held every New Year's Day and features creative floats made from flowers and other organic materials, such as grains of rice, cranberries, and dried coconut used to fill in faces or backgrounds. Sparky invited his daughter Amy to sit with him in a convertible as they waved to the crowd along the five-mile parade route. After that, his strip about the experience showed the amusing truth of how kids rarely recognize their parents' achievements.

Sparky's new wife, Jeannie, realized that Sparky had his own way of doing things. She hoped she could persuade him to travel with her, because she loved exploring other countries. But traveling made him nervous. He preferred to stay home and work

in his studio or sit at the Warm Puppy and see all the people who came there. That's what made him happy. And it fit with his philosophy that it was important to "Be who you are!"

Jeannie quickly realized she was not going to change her husband. If their marriage was going to work, she would have to accept him the way he was.

In 1980, Jeannie and Sparky built a new home in the foothills above Santa Rosa with a beautiful view of the sky, the surrounding hills, and the Pacific Ocean beyond. Every day, Sparky followed his routine in the office at One Snoopy Place: answering the mail, making phone calls, then sitting at his drawing board doodling, as he waited for that day's idea to come into his mind.

Often Sparky interrupted his routine to give interviews to other cartoonists and newspaper people. He was extremely generous about giving advice to cartoonists just starting out. He remembered how much that had meant to him when he was beginning. He answered his mail from young fans, and one day, even picked up the phone to find a third-grade reporter eager to interview him.

Sparky regretted he had not attended college. On his own, he read the classics, new novels, and history books. He also read biographies, especially about musicians rather than artists. He liked to discuss them with friends and with his son, Monte, who had become a novelist. Sparky took classes, mainly in English literature, and read many literary masterpieces. For his classes, he wrote papers about those books. If he got an A on a paper, he bragged to his children and proudly asked them to read what he had written.

Throughout his life, Sparky had studied the Bible and could quote it from memory. He often used Biblical phrases in the strip. Once he showed Linus loosely quoting from the Bible as he and Sally are drenched by the rain. Both of them are wearing raincoats, but Snoopy lies on top of his dog house, complaining that the rain is falling on his face!

(TEN)

Staring Out the Window

Sparky used events from his life in his cartoon strips. When he was worried about the meaning of his life, he drew Snoopy worrying about the meaning in his life. When he was lonely, he drew Charlie Brown feeling lonely.

Sparky also used the strip as a way to honor holidays or other special historical dates. He had served his country as a young infantryman in the army, and he felt that the experience had strengthened him physically and emotionally. The D-Day invasion on June 6, 1944, was an important date to him and to all his buddies. It had been the turning point in World War II when the United States and the Allies surprised Germany and landed thousands of soldiers on the coast of Normandy, France. The invasion helped to end the war.

For the fiftieth anniversary of the invasion, in June 1994, Sparky decided to draw a special Sunday strip, because that would allow enough space to tell the story. He started by reading books and articles about the history of D-Day. He studied photographs about the invasion. He wanted to get every detail exactly right. He even studied photographs of English telephone booths!

For almost a month, he puzzled over the best way to portray this important event in U.S. history. Then, during his research, he discovered a wonderful fact: The general in charge of Germany's forces, the brilliant Field Marshal Erwin Rommel, was leaving Normandy on June 5, the day before the invasion, to celebrate his wife's birthday at home in Germany. Rommel would not be in France where the secret invasion was to take place. "Aha!" thought Sparky. Now he knew how to tell the story.

Not every strip Sparky created required research. Many of them came to him out of the blue. Sometimes an idea popped into his mind while he walked to his studio after breakfast. Or in the middle of the night. Or in the shower. Or while he was doodling at his drawing board. He could never predict when an idea would hatch. One day he might think of ten good ideas. The next day he might not be able to think of a single idea. "It's hard to convince people when you're just staring out of the window that you're doing your hardest work of the day," he said.

101

He liked to plan the strips for the week as a whole. That meant ideas for six strips plus the larger Sunday strip, every single week. Maybe he would use a baseball story or a back-to-school story. He liked to vary the pace in his strips. He felt he could draw a serious subject for one or two days, then the next day Sparky said he might show Snoopy simply watching his friend Woodstock (the bird) bouncing up and down.

"I have a good group," he said. The characters worked well together. He could choose any one of them to create a story. He said that drawing a strip every single day meant you had to "use everything you know, everything you read, everything that happens to you." Often he worked on future strips in case he got sick and couldn't work for a day or two.

Sparky prided himself on always drawing and writing his own strips. He was the only cartoonist who managed to do that for fifty years. He tried to keep his drawings simple and "pleasant to look at." And always funny. He once told an interviewer that he wanted to be remembered for making people happy.

At first, Sparky felt that his drawing was more important than the writing, but then he changed his mind. He realized that his writing was equally important.

Because he never used swear words, Sparky coined his own unique phrases to show his characters' strong feelings: A determined Lucy, who was often frustrated, might shout "Rats!" Or a disappointed Charlie Brown might sigh and mutter, "Good grief." Or a sensitive Linus might wrap himself in his security blanket and say nothing. ("Security blanket" even ended up in the dictionary.)

No matter where Sparky lived, his work was influenced by the changing seasons of his Midwestern childhood. In the spring, the kids were out on the baseball diamond, trying to win a game. At the same time, Charlie Brown was trying to fly a kite, which usually got caught in a tree. Each fall, Lucy would hold up the football for Charlie Brown and pull the ball away just as he was about to kick it. (Good grief!) And of course, each fall in both the comic strip and the Halloween television program, Linus could be found in the pumpkin patch waiting for the Great Pumpkin to appear.

The team rarely won a baseball game. Charlie Brown never had a chance to kick the football or fly the kite, and the Great Pumpkin never appeared. But that didn't mean the kids would stop trying to win or fly or kick or wait. Their determination kept them going and left the reader with the hope that things might change for the better. After all, Sparky had to wait until he was seventy-two to make his first hole-in-one on the golf course.

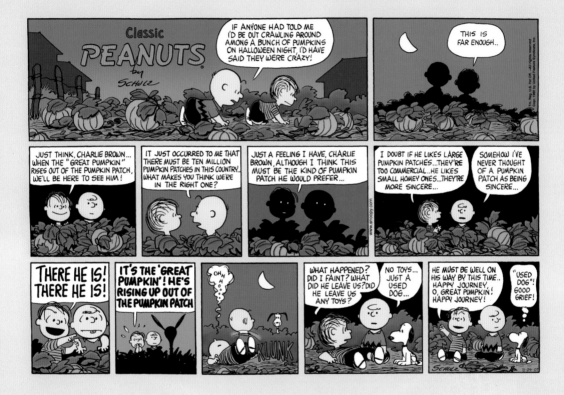

(ELEVEN)

Drawing on the Wall

Throughout his life, Sparky may have collected insults, but those were out-numbered by his awards. Beginning with the Reuben trophies, he won Emmys for his television shows, a Peabody Award for a 1983 television special, a star on the Hollywood Walk of Fame, induction into the Cartoonist Hall of Fame, and many more. He might have explained that his honors were important, but his insults were funnier.

Sparky once told an Ohio journalist, "I'm a little bit of all the characters because that's what I draw. I used to be more Lucy than I am now . . . but I've learned to temper my sarcastic remarks." Charlie Brown, the central character, is usually in a quandary. He reflects Sparky's insecurity and his perseverance. Lucy has his insight and sometimes his anger. Linus has his curiosity and inquisitiveness. Schroeder, his wisdom as well as his love of classical music. Snoopy is the daredevil Sparky wanted to be—the lover, famous author, war hero, and always the dreamer. Readers, too, may find their own personality quirks in the strips. Sparky could control and develop all his characters, but he could not always control his own physical condition. In September 1981, Sparky had open-heart surgery after the doctor told him he had blocked arteries that would prevent him from playing ice hockey, tennis, or golf—all the activities he loved. At first, he was scared just thinking about being cut open and having his heart repaired. He almost decided not to do it. But then he realized he wanted to continue all his activities, and that meant he had to go ahead with the surgery.

For a few days after the surgery, Sparky was quite weak. The doctor told Sparky he had to get out of bed and move around, and he also had to blow into a spirometer to clear out his lungs and prevent any complications, such as pneumonia.

One day, when one of his nurses asked him to draw Snoopy on the wall of his room, he told her he was not strong enough. But Sparky could never turn off his imagination, and in the middle of the night he had an idea. The next morning, he picked up the felt-tip pen his nurse had left on the nightstand, and started drawing a life-sized version of Snoopy on the wall, taking a deep breath and trying to "blow, blow, blow" hard enough to make the small balls in the

SPARKY WITH CHARLIE BROWN, LUCY, AND SNOOPY AS HIS STAR IS PLACED ON HOLLYWOOD BOULEVARD / JUNE 28, 1996

spirometer rise to the top of the tube. He knew that future patients in that hospital room would share his and Snoopy's experience: it hurts to exercise your lungs after surgery. Sparky hoped his drawing might inspire them to keep blowing even though it hurt, and to keep laughing, which would also help their recovery.

Gradually, Sparky was able to resume the strips and play tennis and golf and ice-skate. In the '80s he didn't have the same energy he had when he was younger, and he complained about that, but he was still able to play rugged ice hockey with his team and to come up with new insights for the kids in *Peanuts*. In the '80s he experimented by breaking away from three or four panels to try one long panel. Sometimes he used a single caption instead of speech balloons. And he always worked hard to make the strips better and more interesting.

His own life was changing, too. In 1974, daughter Meredith had a child, Sparky's first grandchild. Sparky had enjoyed his own children, and now they were all having children. Shortly after his surgery, Craig's wife gave birth to a grandson. Over the years,

Amy and her husband had nine children and brought all of them to visit Sparky. She said he was wonderful for about an hour, drawing Snoopys and playing blocks. Then he had to get back to his life and the strip.

He began including stories about wise grand-fathers in the strips, even though they were off the page, just as the parents and teachers had been. Sparky said there "was no room for adults" in his strips. They were too tall to fit in the space, and they didn't belong to the kids' world. But he could have Charlie Brown talk about his dad who loved being a barber, or Linus talk about his great-grandfather who always came early to ball games. It was a way he could add the generations and point to the way life used to be.

Sparky himself didn't like "being old." He didn't like having a tremor in his drawing hand, or not being able to keep up with all the young people at the skating rink, or with his busy family.

In mid-November 1999, Sparky, in terrible pain from a blocked abdominal artery, was rushed to the hospital. His doctors discovered that he had

advanced colon cancer. He was still in the hospital through Thanksgiving and his seventy-seventh birthday on November 26. He decided to retire from creating the strip so that he could deal with his medical problems. As readers heard about his illness, they sent affectionate fan letters to Sparky. Huge bags of mail arrived in his office every day.

After having created nearly 18,000 strips in more than 2,600 newspapers around the world, Sparky's final cartoon strip appeared on Sunday, February 13, 2000.

Sparky died in his sleep on the night of February 12, the night before his final strip appeared. He had accomplished his dream by becoming one of the best cartoonists of his time, drawing the funny pictures that made people happy every single day.

Facing page / SPARKY DRAWING CHARLIE BROWN / C. 1978
Next page / SPARKY'S FINAL STRIP, FEBRUARY 13, 2000

PEANUTS

by SCHULZ

THINK HE'S WRITING..

BONK!

PSYCHIATRIC HELP 5¢

THE DOCTOR IS [IN]

Dear Friends,
   I have been fortunate to draw Charlie Brown and his friends for almost 50 years. It has been the fulfillment of my childhood ambition.
   Unfortunately, I am no longer able to maintain the schedule demanded by a daily comic strip. My family does not wish Peanuts to be continued by anyone else,

WHILE IT'S RAINING..

AAUGH!

CLOMP!

EXTRA CREDIT ON A D-MINUS?

YOU ARE UNCOMMONLY WEIRD, MARCIE!

therefore I am announcing my retirement.

I have been grateful over the years for the loyalty of our editors and the wonderful support and love expressed to me by fans of the comic strip.

Charlie Brown, Snoopy, Linus, Lucy...how can I ever forget them...

Charles M. Schulz

BIBLIOGRAPHY

Books

Bang, Derrick with Victor Lee. *50 Years of Happiness: A Tribute to Charles Schulz*. Peanuts Collector Club.1999.

Inge, M. Thomas, ed. *Charles M. Schulz: Conversations*. Jackson: University Press of Mississippi, October 2000.

Johnson, Rheta Grimsley. *Good Grief: The Story of Charles M. Schulz*. New York: Pharos Books, 1989.

Michaelis, David. *Schulz and Peanuts*. New York: Harper, October 2007.

Schulz, Charles M. *Around the World in 45 Years*. Kansas City, Missouri: United Feature Syndicate, Inc., October 1994.

———. *Charlie Brown, Snoopy and Me: And all the other Peanuts Characters*. Edited by R. Smith Kiliper. New York: Doubleday & Company, Inc. 1980.

———. *The Complete Peanuts*. Edited by Gary Groth. Seattle: Fantagraphics Books, 2004.

———. *Peanuts Jubilee: My Life and Art with Charlie Brown and Others*. New York: Holt, Rinehart and Winston, 1975.

———. *Peanuts: The Art of Charles M. Schulz*. Edited by Chip Kidd. New York: Pantheon Books, 2001.

Schuman, Michael A. *Charles M. Schulz: Cartoonist and Creator of Peanuts*. Berkeley Heights, New Jersey: Enslow Publishers, Inc., March 2002.

Magazines and Newspapers

Curiel, Jonathan and Pamela J. Podger. "Farewell to Schulz, Peanuts." *San Francisco Chronicle*, February 14, 2000, A-1.

Groth, Gary, ed. *The Comics Journal*, No. 290 (1998): 26–111.

Miller, Johnny. "Charles Schulz Moved to California in 1958." San Francisco Chronicle, January 20, 2008, N-60.

Author Interviews

Jeannie Schulz (wife of Charles M. Schulz), various interviews, November 11, 2006–December 20, 2008.

Monte Schulz (son of Charles M. Schulz), May 14, 2007.

Amy Schulz Johnson (daughter of Charles M. Schulz), January 4, 2008.

Jill Schulz Transki (daughter of Charles M. Schulz), March 6, 2008.

Television Programs

American Masters Series. "Good 'Ol Charles Schulz," first broadcast on October 29, 2007, by PBS. A Lumiere, *tpt*, and Thirteen/WNET production, directed by David Van Taylor.

A Charlie Brown Christmas, first broadcast on December 9, 1965, by CBS. Directed by Bill Meléndez and written by Charles M. Schulz.

It's The Great Pumpkin, Charlie Brown, first broadcast on October 27, 1966, by CBS. Directed by Bill Meléndez and written by Charles M. Schulz.

Unpublished Material

Hnidkova, Alena, PhD. "Remembering Charles Schulz," (undated).

Shanahan, Dan. "Critique of *Schulz and Peanuts* by David Michaelis," (undated).

Index

Page numbers in italics indicate photos.

A PROGRESSION OF SNOOPY